Published by
Walker Publishing Company, Inc., New York
Distributed to the trade by
Holtzbrinck Publishers

Library of Congress Cataloging-in-Publication Data
has been applied for.

ISBN-10: 0-8027-1635-0
ISBN-13: 978-0-8027-1635-4

Visit Walker & Company's Web site
at www.walkerbooks.com

First U.S. edition 2007

3 5 7 9 10 8 6 4 2

Designed and typeset by
Wooden Books Ltd, Glastonbury, UK

Printed in the United States of America

ISLAMIC DESIGN

A GENIUS FOR GEOMETRY

Daud Sutton

Walker & Company
New York

WOODEN BOOKS

*In the Name of God,
the Infinitely Good, the All-Merciful.*

This book is dedicated to Dr. Martin Lings, much loved and greatly missed.

*Special thanks to Professor Keith Critchlow for opening the door and
continuing to inspire, to Paul Marchant for all the teaching and ongoing
support, and to Faarid Gouverneur for years of insight and guidance.*

*Thanks are also due to David Apthorp for help with the first draft of this work
during difficult times, to Ahmed Fares for the calligraphy above and on page 13,
and to the team in Cairo and my friends and family for all their support and help.*

If you have enjoyed this book, Professor Keith Critchlow's *Islamic Patterns*,
published by Thames & Hudson, is highly recommended. Also recommended
are *Unity in Pattern* by Paul Marchant, *Arabic Geometrical Pattern and Design* by
J. Burgoin, *Splendours of Qur'an Calligraphy and Illumination* by Dr. Martin
Lings and *Arabesques: Decorative Art in Morocco* by Jean-Marc Castéra.

CONTENTS

Owen Jones' 19th century engraving of the Patio de Comares in Alhambra.

INTRODUCTION

The role of sacred art is to support the spiritual life of those whom it surrounds, to instill a way of perceiving the world and the subtle realities behind it. The challenge thus facing the traditional artisan is how to build with matter so as to best embody spirit. The great temples, churches and mosques of the world are the legacy of our attempts to do just this, each determined by the spiritual perspective in question.

Throughout their long history the craft traditions of the Islamic world evolved a multitude of styles applied to a great variety of media, but always with unifying factors that make them instantly recognizable. It is perhaps no surprise that an art form that seeks explicitly to explore the relationship between Unity and multiplicity should be at the same time unified yet diverse. Harmony is central.

The visual structure of Islamic design has two key aspects: calligraphy using Arabic script – one of the world's great scribal traditions – and abstract ornamentation using a varied but remarkably integrated visual language. This art of pure ornament revolves around two poles: geometric pattern, the harmonic and symmetrical subdivision of the plane giving rise to intricately interwoven designs that speak of infinity and the omnipresent center; and idealized plant form or arabesque, spiraling tendrils, leaves, buds and flowers embodying organic life and rhythm. This book focuses on Islamic geometric patterns, exploring their structure and meaning.

FIRST THINGS FIRST
unfolding from unity

Consider a point, dimensionless position in space. Extending the point defines a line (*below left*). Turning the span of this line about the first point traces a circle, the first and the simplest geometric plane figure and Unity's perfect symbol. Mark a second circle, centered on the circumference of the first and passing through its center. Continue by placing circles at each new intersection to fit six identical circles cycling around a central one, the ideal representation of the Quranic six days of creation. This beautifully simple construction can be continued indefinitely (*opposite*), defining a tessellation of regular hexagons perfectly filling the plane.

The mid-points of a regular hexagon's sides join to form a double triangle (*top right opposite*), known in the Islamic World as the Seal of Solomon – it is said that the ring by which he commanded the *jinn* bore this crest. Repeating the outline of this six-pointed star within each hexagon gives a pattern of stars and hexagons.

The final stage opposite shows the pattern as it is found in the Ibn Tulun Mosque in Cairo (879 C.E.), carved in plaster. The pattern's lines have been rendered as interlacing bands, passing over and under each other where they cross, and the remaining spaces filled with arabesque motifs.

SIXES EXTRAPOLATED

some more basics

Many different techniques of geometric construction have been used throughout the Islamic world, adding practical aids such as set squares, stencils and grids to the fundamental tools of compasses and straight edge. Most of the small selection of constructions in this book use a philosophical method relying solely on compasses and straight edge and emphasizing the geometric underpinning of the patterns as a whole.

Simple patterns lend themselves to adaptation in many ways and the constructions shown opposite develop two variations on the star-and-hexagon pattern from the previous page. The points of intersection in the patterns' paths remain fixed at the midpoints of the hexagonal subgrid's edges, while the stars expand and contract respectively. The same equilateral three-fold hexagons occur in both of these adaptations, yet the two patterns give remarkably different overall impressions.

Below is another example of how simple patterns can extrapolate into more complex ones. Starting again with the star-and-hexagon design, cut four points off some stars to form rhombs (*center*) and remove small hexagons to create a pattern that reads as both individual shapes and large overlapping hexagons (*right*).

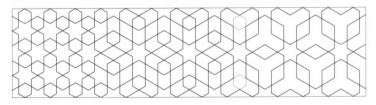

Starting with six circles around one, add six more at the outer vertices.

Join the marked points. The hexagonal repeat (shaded) contains the first circle.

The basic star-and-hexagon pattern can be traced on this substructure.

The substructure's vertices give a section of an alternative pattern (repeated below)

Add lines joining the points marked to define a small proportioning circle

The vertices now defined give a section of the second alternative pattern (repeated below).

Transforming a Subgrid
and framing the infinite

The construction on the previous page also defines a semiregular tiling of equilateral triangles, squares, and regular hexagons (*left, top row*). Notice that this design, when repeated (*right, top row*), is itself underpinned by the regular tiling of hexagons (*dotted line*).

Picture the triangles in the pattern inflating as the hexagons are pinched, the squares giving exactly as much as they take. When the triangles have become the same equilateral three-fold hexagons as on the previous page, a beautiful pattern of overlapping regular dodecagons is defined (*left, middle row*). Continuing until the triangles form regular hexagons gives a second frequently encountered pattern (*right, middle row*).

Conceptually a repeating pattern can continue forever, but in practical applications Islamic patterns are generally cropped to form rectangular sections with corners in the center of key pieces, often stars (*bottom row, opposite*). Framing a pattern this way maintains a geometric elegance at the same time as clearly implying that it could repeat indefinitely, as it were, under its borders – the perfect visual solution to calling to mind the idea of infinity, and hence the Infinite, without any pretence of being able to truly capture such an enigmatic concept visually.

This framing also usually gives a single central piece which ensures that the total number of pieces in the rectangle is odd – a numerical quality traditionally said to invoke, and find favor with, Divine Unity.

GIVE AND TAKE
the breath of the compassionate

Start with a circle set on a horizontal line and trace arcs centered on and passing through the intersections to define a vertical (*below left*). Repeating this on the new intersections defines diagonals on which four circles, identical to the first, can be drawn. Add four more circles to produce an array of eight around one. As with the pattern on page 3 this circular matrix can be continued indefinitely to define a tessellation, this time of squares (*opposite*).

Combining a horizontal square with a diagonal one produces an eight-pointed star (*top right opposite*). Like the double triangle this double square is known as the Seal (*khātam* in Arabic) of Solomon, for the legends vary, and is the starting point of a vast family of patterns (*see page 26*). Repeating them in each square makes the fundamental pattern of stars and crosses opposite.

This pattern can also be seen as a tiling of smaller diagonal squares, half of which expand and the other half of which contract. For this reason it has, in recent times, been referred to as *The Breath of The Compassionate*, a name referring to the teachings of the Great Master Ibn al-'Arabī which expound the Divine Breath as the basis of creation, liberating the possibilities of the four Elements; Fire, Air, Water and Earth.

9

EIGHT-FOLD ROSETTES
and some construction principles

A prevalent device in Islamic geometric patterns is the distinctive geometric rosette, with its petals arranged around a central star like an archetypal crystalline flower. Rosette patterns such as these can also be seen as a network of stellar motifs, inverting perception to picture the petals as negative space. Shown here are eight-fold rosettes rendered in a style based on carpentry panels.

Two methods of construction are shown. Below is a simple one based on a square grid; here the large regular octagon is defined by diagonals and a circle, and partitioned into the geometric rosette with petals one quarter the width of the whole square repeat. Opposite is another that ensures the points of the five-pointed stars, two halves of which are set on each side of the square, all lie on the same circle. This makes the four short edges of the hexagonal petals identical in length, a geometric subtlety particularly common in carpentry applications.

The other patterns opposite show some of the ways that the shapes generated in the simple rosette can be rearranged, giving rise to new shapes in the process. Repeating sections are not restricted to squares only, but include carefully proportioned rectangles.

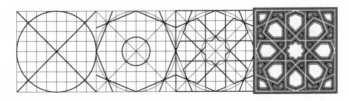

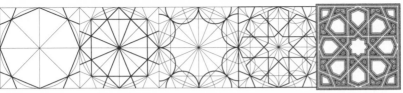

Place a circle and both diagonals within a quartered square to define an octagon.

Adding a double square octagram defines one sixteenth radial divisions.

Trace arcs as shown centered where the one sixteenth division radii cut the square.

These arcs intersect the radii to define the rosette's petals and central star

A single repeat unit rendered as it might appear as a simple carpentry panel.

A variation in a rectangle with sides in the ratio 1:√2.

Rotated one sixteenth of a turn and set in a larger square.

A curious variation using the petals and small octagons.

A large composition showing the harmonious interaction of the small octagons and the eight-fold rosettes.

The central vertical section of the pattern to the left tiled as a repeat unit, two shown here.

CALLIGRAPHY
the proportioned alphabet

Quran literally means *recitation*, for initially the Holy Book was memorized by heart. Soon, however, it became necessary to record it in written form and the hitherto rudimentary Arabic script became the focus for generations of devoted scribes striving to develop the most suitable hands for the scripture.

The first truly Quranic script to be used (*ca.* 9th C. C.E.) is termed Kufic, after the town of Kufa in Iraq. Predominantly horizontal in movement, its commanding presence conveys majesty and austerity (*below*). Many ornamental scripts were derived from Kufic (*see page 57*) and remained in use long after the original hand.

The most well known styles of Arabic calligraphy today are the cursive scripts. Their refined form originated in the inspired system of proportioning developed by Ibn Muqla (d. 940 C.E.), prior to which they held a relatively low profile in relation to the majestic Kufic. Here the fundamental starting points of geometry also underpin calligraphic form – every letter is carefully proportioned in relation to the circle, its diameter, and the point, or *nuqta*, marked as a rhombic dot with the reed pen. The first and most fundamental letter is the *alif*, traced as an elegant vertical stroke within the circle. Different systems of proportioning the *alif* exist, using six, seven, or eight vertically spaced *nuqāt*.

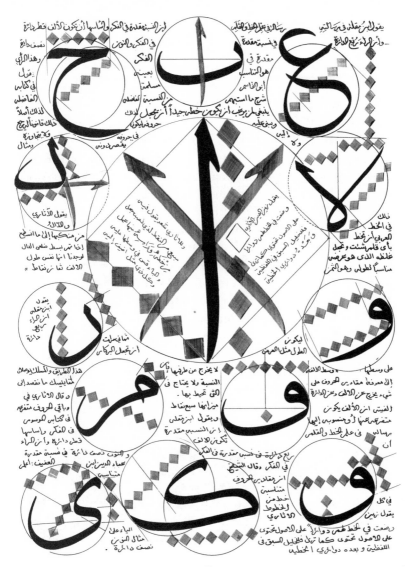

ARABESQUE
the gardens of paradise

Arabesque designs, *islīmī* in Persian, are the complement of geometric patterns. They aim not to imitate the plant kingdom naturalistically but to distill visually the essence of rhythm and growth it manifests, recalling the archetypal Gardens of Paradise. Varied arabesque styles (*opposite*) are one of the more obvious differences between regions and eras of Islamic design.

Spirals are primordial and universal symbols, intimately related to life and its cycles. They embody the eddying process of Creation's expansion and contraction and find their application in Islamic design as the basis for many arabesque motifs. Designs such as the one below are often found winding behind Quranic text, in friezes and the title panels of illuminated books. When used this way the vine continues behind the letters while the leaves and flowers fill the remaining spaces.

The spiral is associated worldwide with the sun and its yearly cycle. The sun unwinds from its rebirth at the winter solstice, loops ever more widely in the sky, past the balance points of the equinox to the summer solstice, when it is sky borne for the longest period in its cycle, before winding back up to its midwinter demise.

A 9th century arabesque design in marble relief, from the great mosque in Kairouan, Tunisia.

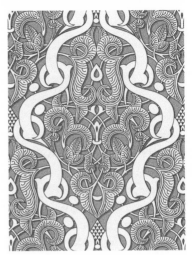

A repeating arabesque design in carved plaster from Alhambra in a typically Maghribi style.

Ottoman arabesque from underglaze Iznik tiles in rich dark blue, turquoise, green, and red

A highly geometric arabesque design from Cairo, trellised by the pattern on page 36.

SIX OF ONE
half a dozen of the other

Start with the basic star-and-hexagon pattern (*below left*) and rotate each star through one twelfth of a full turn (*below center*). Extend the lines of these stars' corners to form small triangles to create a basic pattern of twelve-fold stars (*below right*).

Illustrated opposite is the generation of a pattern based on the semiregular tiling of regular dodecagons, regular hexagons and squares. Stars are set within the subgrid's shapes, with points of sixty degrees touching the midpoints of each edge. As below, the twelve-pointed star is made from two overlapping six-fold stars.

The star points of Islamic patterns often touch to form two intersecting line segments making over-under interlacing, as used opposite, an easily applied articulation. Appropriately, geometric patterns are known in Persian as *girih*, literally knots, calling to mind weaving and the talismanic effect of knots and braids. A pattern with interlacing strap work no longer has mirror symmetry; reflecting it turns all the "overs" into "unders" and vice versa.

The world's spiritual traditions are in agreement that what we see of the world rests on an unseen, subtle and meaningful order. Likewise, the subgrid and implicit circles of patterns like that opposite are openly concealed in the finished design, hidden in plain view by the clothing through which they can be perceived.

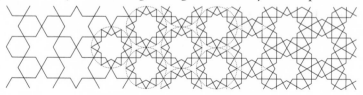

THREE TIMES FOUR
and four times three

From the disciples of Christ to the months of the canonical lunar year the number twelve has many associations in Islam. Twelve is the first *abundant number*, a number whose factors sum to more than itself: 1+2+3+4+6=16. These factors also all occur in either the hexagonal or square repeat systems, making twelve-fold motifs particularly useful in pattern making.

The diagrams opposite explore the family of patterns introduced on the previous page. The basic pattern of twelve-fold stars is shown unfolding from the semiregular tiling of regular dodecagons and triangles (*opposite top*). Notice the way that the finished pattern can be seen as overlapping large hexagons and interwoven zigzags.

Arranging dodecagons edge to edge on a square repeat gives the second subgrid opposite. The star pattern created from this subgrid can be seen as overlapping octagons with interlaced paths.

Take the arrangement of four triangles around a square from the second subgrid and use it to space dodecagons in a triangular repeat to create the third subgrid opposite. The spaces left form the same three-fold hexagons as on page 5 (*below, fourth shape*).

This third subgrid can be extrapolated into a fourth, arranged in a square repeat. Adding the relevant stars creates a particularly sophisticated pattern. Note the dodecagonal paths around the twelve-pointed stars in both the third and fourth patterns.

FURTHER TWELVES
and some rosette constructions

Generating patterns by the interplay of square and hexagonal repeat structures with twelve-fold motifs is not limited to the previous examples. For example, shown opposite are a pattern from a door panel in the Christian quarter of Damascus and a variation on this by Paul Marchant. Their underlying structures are shown below; groups of three squares forming twelve-fold stars are set respectively on square (*left*) and triangular (*right*) grids – the dotted lines show the sections used in the illustrations. Dedicated geometers will note that the corners of the squares (*marked opposite as black dots*) define lines that give the rest of the points needed to develop the full pattern (*white dots*). These lines also extend to give the proportion of the central stars within the rosettes.

The same rosette proportions can be established independently of the pattern, as depicted opposite with two more rosette constructions. All three constructions start from a double hexagon set within a regular dodecagon with radial lines added. Black dots mark key points that are found in the initial structure, gray dots mark any intermediary points needed, and white dots mark the points that give the final proportions of the star.

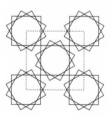 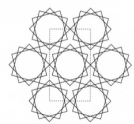

Source pattern from Damascus with square repeat
above. Triangular repeat variation opposite.

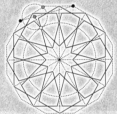

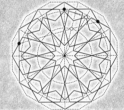

The rosette used above,
proportioned from its outer structure.

A rosette constructed to make
the petals' four short edges equal.

Narrow petals with an
additional harmonious star added.

The rosettes above, plus a fourth variation, placed within a square repeat framework from Alhambra.

21

THREE-FOLD PERMUTATIONS
multiples from the matrix

Most of the patterns covered so far repeat on either a regular hexagonal or square grid, and a more systematic look at the hexagonal grid is shown below. Joining the centers of the hexagons defines a regular tiling of equilateral triangles – these two grids are each other's duals. Any pattern that can be repeated with regular hexagons can also be repeated with equilateral triangles.

The smallest section needed to define an entire hexagonal repeat pattern is one of the light gray or white triangles below. These triangles have sides in the ratio $1:\sqrt{3}:2$ ($\sqrt{3}$ is approximately 1.732) and this structure is sometimes called the $\sqrt{3}$ system. By rotating, reflecting, and translating (sliding) one of these triangles it is possible to generate the entire pattern. Some traditional methods construct a stencil of such a triangle and apply these three symmetry movements to complete the pattern.

The points where three hexagonal repeats meet have shapes with rotational symmetry in multiples of three, and the points where six triangular repeats meet have shapes with rotational symmetry in multiples of six (*opposite top left*). These multiples permute to give different numbers at these key points. Each illustration opposite shows the same portion of a pattern in relation to the subgrid.

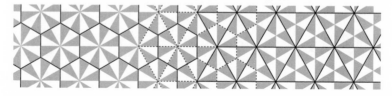

22

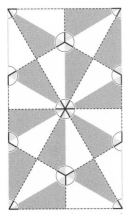

A 1:√3 rectangular section made of 1 hexagon and 4 quarter hexagons, or, 2 triangles and 4 half triangles.

A Seljuk design with wide strap work. Threes and sixes, in this case triangles and six-pointed stars, lie on the key points.

Twelve-fold rosettes with three-fold equilateral hexagons. All the petal shapes, in the rosettes and between them, are identical.

A Maghribi, or western, pattern, based on the semiregular grid at the top of page 17, with twelve and six at the key points.

A sophisticated Mamluk design, three times three gives nine at the three-fold key points, with six on the others.

A pattern combining fifteen, five times three, with twelve, two times six. For nine and twelve see the cover of this book.

FOUR-FOLD PERMUTATIONS
quadruples in quadrangles

Joining the centers of squares set in a regular tiling defines another square tiling – the square grid is its own dual. The smallest section needed to define a whole square repeat pattern is one of the light gray or white triangles below. These triangles have sides in the ratio $1:1:\sqrt{2}$ ($\sqrt{2}$ is approximately equal to 1.414) and this structure is sometimes known as the $\sqrt{2}$ system. As with the hexagonal system, rotating, reflecting, and translating this minimum section can generate an entire pattern.

Two minimum triangles, long edge to long edge, form a square and with so many squares to choose from it can sometimes be tricky to distinguish the two dual grids and the minimum section triangles in a square repeat pattern. In addition, the size of a pattern's pieces relative to the repeat can vary considerably. However, with a little practice these structures can be discerned quite easily.

In square repeat patterns the points where four squares meet have shapes with rotational symmetry in multiples of four, but, as there are two dual square grids to consider, different multiples can be combined (*opposite top left*). Opposite are some of the ways these multiples permute, each illustration showing the same portion of a pattern in relation to the subgrid.

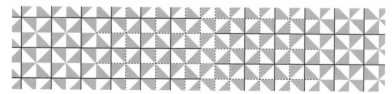

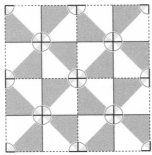

Dual square grids, dotted and solid, and the key four-fold points.

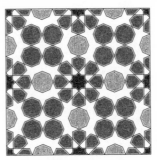

Eight, two times four, and four, in a pattern related to those on page 11.

Another elegant pattern combining eight and four, at the key points, with six.

Twelve and four in the square repeat version of a fundamental pattern.

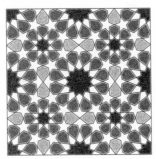

Twelve and eight, the petals are the same shape as on page 23, top right.

Sixteen and four at the key points, with eights in between.

PIECES OF EIGHT
barbary brilliance

Over the centuries artisans in the Maghrib, the West of the Islamic world, explored a remarkable form-language based on the square repeat and, in particular, the possibilities inherent in the eight-fold *khātam*. The *Breath of the Compassionate* is shown below unfolding from the semiregular tiling of octagons and squares. Tracing octagram stars by joining every third corner within each *khātam* creates a simple pattern using this set of shapes.

Opposite is an example of the way simple geometric relationships build upon each other from an initial square grid to generate a whole series of different square repeat patterns. The shapes that arise from generating these patterns are collected in the central panel. Together with many other related shapes they are cut to this day in Morocco in brightly colored friable tiles to create a vast puzzle set with countless solutions.

The two-fold hexagon found third down in the left hand column of the central panel opposite, known as a *ṣaft*, is a particularly important shape in this system. The *ṣaft* plays a fundamental role in the generation of more complex *zillīj* patterns such as the one covered on the following page.

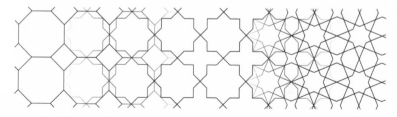

27

ZILLĪJ DESIGN
eight-fold extravaganzas

The cut tile work of the Maghrib is known as *zillīj*. The medieval glaze palette for this work was limited to only a few colors; black, white, dark green, turquoise, blue, and a warm yellow ochre. Nowadays many other colors are also used.

Vast compositions can be made with *zillīj*, compiled in a modular technique that alternates *khātam* with *ṣaft* to make a framework of sections to fill (*black pieces opposite*). Rings of color are arranged within these sections to create designs that read well to the eye from far away, when geometric detail can no longer be seen, and close up, where individual shapes are clear. Note the way that the same shape occurs in different tones in the design.

The rosettes used opposite have twenty-four and sixteen petals, requiring the construction of pieces that interface with the eight-fold geometry. Although asymmetric these pieces read comfortably in context, perhaps because of their geometric necessity.

Zillīj can be composed on paper using a simple square grid (*below*), sketching approximations of the forms before assembling the final work with correctly cut tile pieces. This method works by replacing the √2 ratio of a square's diagonal to its side, found in the correct shapes, with the fractions 3/2 (1.5) and 7/5 (1.4).

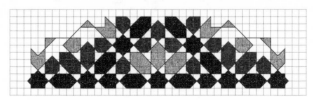

28

29

SELF-SIMILARITY
the same at different scales

Mathematicians use the term *fractal* to refer to mathematical objects that exhibit self-similarity, with the same forms and patterns occurring at many different scales. Fractals embody infinity through the endless recurrence of similar structures, rather than the unbounded continuation of repeating pattern. This concept has long been used in some aspects of Islamic design.

The panel opposite is based on *zillīj* found in the Alcázar in Seville. A complex web of interlaced white strap work contains the familiar *zillīj* shapes in blue, green, ochre and black. Remarkably, these shapes then form large versions of themselves, outlined in black. This design also contains a third level of implicit self-similarity – the interlacing strap work is proportioned exactly as if it too rested on even smaller *zillīj* pieces (*opposite below*). It seems the designers of this pattern were well aware of the possibility of this subdivision continuing indefinitely.

Self-similar designs such as this are not limited to eight-fold *zillīj*; the families of forms derived from ten-fold geometry (*pages 34 to 37*) are also eminently suited to this type of composition. Self-similarity also occurs in arabesque designs, with leaf forms composed of interconnected smaller leaves and vines (*below*).

ARCING PATTERNS
the balance of line and curve

Not all Islamic patterns leave circles hidden within their implicit construction. Geometric designs that combine arcs and straight lines in their final forms have been a feature of the art form since its beginning. They are usually found rendered in materials that are relatively easy to form into curved shapes, such as the painted arts of the book, metalwork, and carved stone. Patterns using arcs have a distinctly softer appeal, on occasion giving the impression of merging with the arabesque designs their pieces may contain.

The pattern below is from a carved stone window grille in the great Umayyad mosque of Damascus (715 C.E.). Straight bands form the semiregular tiling of regular hexagons and equilateral triangles. Interlaced with these are sections of circles centered on the triangles' vertices and passing two thirds of the way along their sides.

The design opposite is based on a pattern given to Professor Keith Critchlow. The arabesque motifs filling the spaces are in the style of Mamluk Quran illumination. These two patterns are an excellent example of the way that the subgrids used, often quite obvious in early patterns, are more fully concealed in later work.

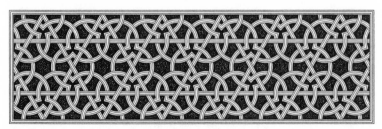

TEN-FOLD TILING
a family of forms

Unlike triangles, squares and hexagons, regular pentagons cannot be arranged to fill a flat surface without leaving gaps. As the art of geometric patterns developed in the Islamic world, artisans inevitably turned their attention to this challenge and discovered ingenious ways of creating designs using five- and ten-fold symmetries.

The diagram below shows a pattern unfolding from a subgrid of repeating regular decagons, placed edge to edge to leave curious bowtie-shaped hexagons. Stars are traced from the midpoints of the decagons' edges forming pentagons at the decagons' corners. The lines of the stars extend into the spaces between decagons to complete the pattern. This pattern is known in Persian as *Umm al-Girih*, the mother of patterns (knots), and its component shapes are the first generation in a whole family of forms (*see page 54*).

The constructions shown opposite are based on an Iranian method. Radial lines marking every eighteen degrees (*dotted*) are intersected by additional lines (*solid*) to give proportioning circles. These circles intersect the radial lines in delicate webs that give the vertices of the final pattern. The arabesque motifs used opposite are in the style of Mamluk Quran illumination.

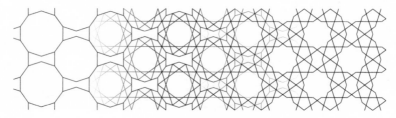

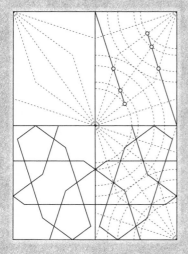

PENTAGRAMMATON
a second ten-fold family

Replace every regular pentagon in the *Umm al-Girih*, including the two overlapping pentagons of the large ten-pointed stars, with five-pointed stars to generate the fundamental pattern of a second ten-fold set of shapes. As with the *Umm al-Girih* this pattern's components are the first generation in a whole family of forms, some of which are shown opposite.

Both of the ten-fold shape-sets can be used to make a countless variety of patterns. For example, the wooden window shutters in the great Ottoman mosques of Istanbul bear a multitude of ten-fold designs, in some buildings seemingly without repetition. Two designs from the Sokullu Mehmet Pasha mosque are illustrated opposite with an example of the symbolism sometimes concealed in the number of a pattern's pieces.

Five-fold and ten-fold geometry embody the elegant golden section, the proportion formed when a line is cut such that the shorter section is to the longer as the longer is to the whole line (approximately 1.618). In the pattern below each distance that can be measured between corners or intersections on a line forms a golden section with the next smallest or next largest distance.

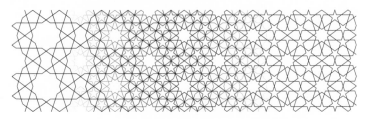

Arabic letters all have numerical values. This system, known as "abjad," was originally used for writing numbers before Indian decimal numerals were adopted. Nowadays it is used for its symbolic value. The pattern above right is composed of 165 pieces, the abjad total for 'La ilaha illa Allah.'– 'There is no divinity but God.' – the quintessential statement of Divine Unity in Islam. A related example is shown in the frontispiece of this book; 99 pieces correspond to the traditional number of Divine Names.

DECIMAL CONNECTIONS
between the two families

The basic ten-fold patterns on the previous pages can also be generated from a subgrid of regular decagons, pentagons and pentagon-based hexagons (*below left*). Placing pentagons and pentagram stars in this subgrid gives the two patterns (*below right*).

Arranging the two patterns this way suggests the possibility of varying the angles formed where paths cross at the subgrid's edge midpoints. The *Umm al-Girih* has angles of 108° at these fixed points, while the other basic ten-fold pattern has angles of 36°. A surprisingly floral design is given by 90° (*top left*), while 72° generates a pattern combining both families of ten-fold forms, an example of how successfully they can be integrated (*top right*). Finally, an angle of 54° produces particularly elegant petal shapes and a small central star the same shape as the first example's central star (*bottom left*).

The final example opposite takes the second variation (*dotted line*) and replaces its rosettes with those found on the previous page, showing just how beautifully harmonious the interrelationships between patterns in these ten-fold form-languages can be.

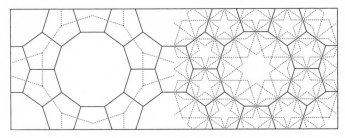

PERFECT FOURTEEN
number of the prophet

The patterns shown here are based on fourteen-fold rosettes, the petals of which fit within the central star in the same way that the petals on page 37 fit within their central ten-fold star. However, the proportions inherent to the heptagram and the tetradecagonal star are more complex than the unique golden section found in the pentagram and the decagonal star, and, as a result, they can easily combine to fall out of synchronization with each other. Patterns in this fourteen-fold family are thus much harder to design successfully and are consequently much rarer. Two basic patterns are shown below. The more intricate pattern shown opposite is rendered as it is found in a carpentry panel at the mausoleum of the Mamluk Sultan Qaytbay (d. 1496 c.e.) in Cairo.

In the Islamic calendar the month begins on the evening of the new crescent's sighting, making the fourteenth of the month the night of the full moon, when the moon reflects the sun's light most fully on the Earth (the moon can also appear full on either the thirteenth or fifteenth). Accordingly the Prophet Muhammad, held to be the mirror of Divine Light within creation, is associated with both the full moon and the number fourteen.

41

SINGULAR STELLATIONS
working with odd numbers

With a few notable exceptions, such as five and seven in ten- and fourteen-fold patterns, or multiples of three, odd numbers, particular prime numbers, are tricky to create patterns with.

A frequently used technique for making patterns with odd numbers is to set the odd-numbered motif along the edges of a square or rectangular section, half on one side and half on the other. This section can then be repeatedly reflected on all sides. A simple example of this technique is shown below; heptagonal stars forming an elegant dancing pattern.

Opposite is a more sophisticated design using nine- and eleven-pointed stars in the style of Persian cut tile work, based on a pattern devised by Jay Bonner. The subgrid for this pattern uses hendecagons and enneagons (*opposite below left*). It can be understood as reflecting rectangular sections (*dotted center*), or, alternatively, an elongated hexagonal repeat joining the centers of six hendecagons (*shaded center*). A similar elongated repeat hexagon can be set on the centers of six enneagons. Two ninths of a full turn, 80°, plus three elevenths of a full turn, approximately 98.2°, is very close to 180°. This allows a rhombic arrangement of two enneagons and two hendecagons (*shaded right*), the nine- and eleven-fold symmetries being almost imperceptibly tweaked to fit together.

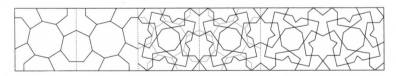

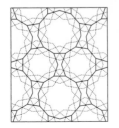
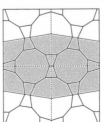

MAKING THINGS FIT
tweaking towards unification

The tweaking technique used on the previous page is not restricted to working with odd numbers – certain remarkable patterns aim to integrate many different numbers as accurately and beautifully as possible. Two examples of this type of pattern are shown opposite with their subgrids. A simpler combination of twelve-, eight-, and approximate five-fold geometry is shown below.

These patterns aspire to reintegrate the multiplicity of number in a harmonious unity, and the connection with harmony is more than just visual analogy. As with the previous pattern using nine- and eleven-fold stars these constructions rest on the fact that the sum of certain fractions is very close, but not equal, to other fractions. Similarly the very first challenge that the student of musical harmony faces in forming a scale is the small discrepancy between multiples and powers of the pure overtone wavelength fractions of $\frac{1}{2}$, $\frac{1}{3}$, $\frac{1}{4}$, $\frac{1}{5}$ and so on. For example, six pure whole tones, $(\frac{8}{9})^6$ (approximately 0.493), falls just short of one octave, $\frac{1}{2}$.

The kite shapes in the pattern below, bridging the space between the stars and defining small quadrilaterals where they overlap, are an example of a frequently used device that occurs in both number-combining patterns and those with one key symmetry.

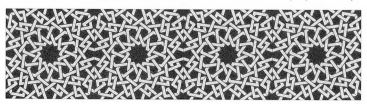

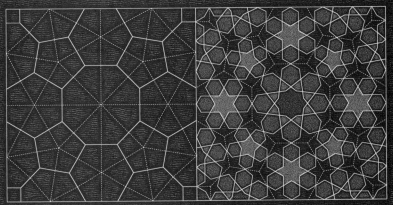

Regular octagons and regular hexagons make a framework into which approximate pentagons and heptagons fit to leave small squares, combining 4, 5, 6, 7, and 8 in one pattern. The important fractional approximations in this construction are $1/5 + 1/6 + 1/8 = 1/2$ (the triangle joining the centers of the 5-, 6-, and 8-gon), and $1/5 + 1/6 + 1/7 = 1/2$ (the triangle joining the centers of the 5-, 6-, and 7-gon).

Regular dodecagons and decagons combine with approximate enneagons to generate a rosette design using 9, 10, and 12. The important fractional approximation in this construction is $2/9 + 3/20 + 3/24 = 1/2$.

DOME GEOMETRY
the third dimension

Islamic architecture is well known for its domed structures. Many architects of these domes were content to present them unadorned, their engineering and elegant form proving sufficient for their goals. But on occasion domes were ornamented with geometric patterns. Well-known examples occur in the monuments of Mamluk Egypt and Safavid Iran – the dome illustrated opposite is from the mausoleum of Sultan Qaytbay in Cairo.

The basic method used in the geometric ornamentation of domes is to repeat sections like the segments of an orange. Stars and interconnecting pieces are placed in these segments and tweaked to fit as the width narrows towards the top (*opposite top left*). Many such domes resolve at the top with petal- and kite-shapes that form rosettes when viewed from above (*opposite top right*).

The true spherical equivalents of the regular and semiregular tilings are the divisions of a sphere that arise from the Platonic and Archimedean solids. There is no well-known evidence of artisans in the Islamic world using these uniquely spherical tilings – they seem to remain a largely unexplored possibility in Islamic design. The example below shows a spherical pattern derived from the cube and regular octahedron, based on work by Craig Kaplan.

MUQARNAS
celestial cascades

Surmounting a square or rectangular structure with a dome necessitates a transitional device, and in time a distinctive solution for this, known as *muqarnas*, arose in Islamic architecture. *Muqarnas* are structured on tiered horizontal layers joined by flat and curved surfaces which articulate their descent – echoing the idea of spiritual light cascading from the Heavens to condense as crystalline matter on Earth. They are also used in niches, for example the niche, or *mihrāb*, that marks the mosque wall facing Mecca.

Muqarnas' functions range from fulfilling structural necessity, for example transferring forces with carved stone in Egypt, Syria, or Turkey, to the purely ornamental articulation of space in the tile-clad structures assembled within the brick architecture of Iran, or the wood and plaster techniques of the Maghrib.

The design of *muqarnas* varies in different regions and eras. In the Maghrib a modular system based on eight-fold geometry proved perfectly at home (*below*). The east of the Islamic world employs *muqarnas* with concentric tiers around a central pole, some designs using different stars on each tier, others using stalactite forms within curved bays (*opposite*), and yet others emphasizing a triangular, prism-like articulation between tiers.

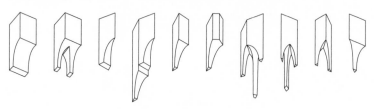

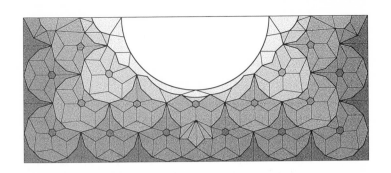

CLOSING THOUGHTS
and further possibilities

Traditional Islamic ornament is eminently functional – but its function is not utilitarian. It seeks to compensate for the spiritual losses of civilization by re-establishing something of the primordial beauty of virgin nature, and to transport the viewer from immersion in the mundane to serene contemplation. Islamic design can be thought of as a form of visual music; the repetition and rhythm of its motifs establish an inner sense of balance and act as a visual extension of the invocatory remembrance of the Divine.

The simplicity and apparent inevitability with which many Islamic geometric patterns unfold belie the effort involved in finding them. The anonymous artisans concerned must surely have regarded them as preexistent possibilities gifted from the Source to those who proved worthy. Not a few such craftsmen must have been well aware of the *abjad* equality between the words "point," *nuqta,* and "geometer," *muhandis*, and aspired to allow this transcendent relationship to shine through in their works.

The design opposite is based on a variation on a theme by Paul Marchant, marrying forms from the two interrelated ten-fold families. At the close of this small book it is a fitting reminder that possibilities yet remain open for exploration in the art of making Islamic geometric patterns.

ONE- & TWO-PIECE PATTERNS

The patterns below are all made of only one or two different shapes and are constructed on either a square grid or a triangular grid. They can all be drawn relatively easily on squared graph paper or isometric paper, or alternatively only require one or two stencils, making them ideal for use in the classroom. Some vertices in the square patterns lie midway between grid intersections. The two curved patterns use the compasses to trace arcs centered on, and passing through, points on their grids. The coloring schemes can vary from those shown.

53

AN INFINITE PUZZLE SET

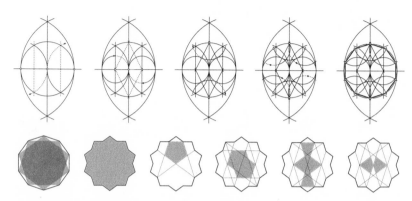

The *Umm al-Girih* is the starting point for a whole range of patterns. An excellent way to explore these patterns is to make a puzzle set of pieces. Follow the diagrams above to construct a regular decagon – a radius of about 2" is a suitable size for the first circle – and then derive each shape from this decagon; star, pentagon, "merged" double pentagon, "bottle," and "kite." Make a stencil for each shape from stiff card or thin plastic and cut out as many pieces as needed from colored card or paper to complete a puzzle set. The possibilities with such a set

are limited only by the number of pieces cut, especially if one starts to explore color schemes or aperiodic and fractal repeat structures. To complete the patterns below, plus those on page 35, cut out the numbers of pieces shown. In order to leave a neat rectangular outline half and quarter shapes need to be cut as detailed. Counting, and maybe even making, the number of pieces needed for the pattern opposite, from the I'timad al-Daula Mausoleum in Agra, India, is left to the enthusiastic reader, or perhaps a classroom full of students.

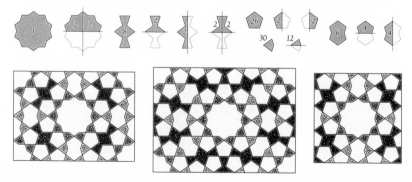

54

SUBGRIDS

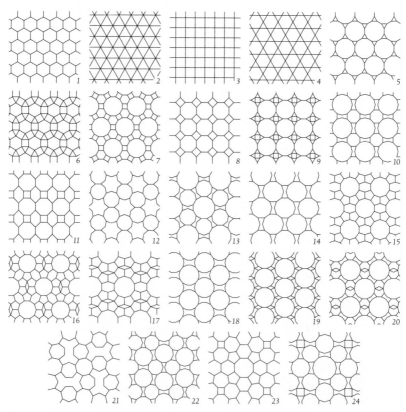

Most patterns in this book rest on relatively simple polygonal subgrids. Those used are shown here with the pages on which they occur: 1. p.3, p.4, p.5 - 2. dual of 1. - 3. p.9, p.25 (*middle left*), p.26 - 4. p.32, p.33 - 5. p.16, p.19 (*top row*), p.21 (*top right*), p.23 (*top center and top right*) - 6. p.7, p. 19 (*third row*) - 7. p.17, p.23 (*bottom left*) - 8. p.9 (*alternative for 3.*), p.25 (*top right and bottom right*), p.26, p.10, p.11 (*top row*) - 9. p.19 (*second*

row and bottom), p.21 (*top left*) - 10. p.25 (*bottom left*), p.44 - 11. p.11 (*second row left*) - 12. p.23 (*bottom middle*) - 13. front cover - 14. p.15 (*bottom right*), p.34, p.35 (*top*), p.36, p.38, p.39 (*all patterns*) - 15. p.15 (*bottom right*), p.34, p.35 (*top*), p.36, p.38, p.39 (*all patterns, alternative for 14.*) - 16. p.35 (*bottom*) - 17. half title page - 18. p.40 (*left*) - 19. p.40 (*right*) - 20. p.41 - 21. p.42 - 22. p.43 - 23. p.45 (*top*) - 24. p.45 (*bottom*).

SQUARE KUFIC

Of all the ornamental styles developed from early Kufic script *Square Kufic*, set rigorously on a square grid, is the most obviously geometric. Alphabetic writing encodes the sounds of speech and thus conveys words, sentences, new information, and, above all, meaning to the reader. Square Kufic presents a curious inversion of this function as it remains well nigh illegible to a great many Arabic readers, its purely graphic twists, turns, simplifications, and compromises to letterform leaving them lost. It is easiest to decipher when the word or phrase written is already well known to the viewer, thus rather than conveying new information, or preserving a text accurately for posterity, Square Kufic acts primarily as a talismanic invocation of sacred words and phrases already familiar. Simple words or phrases are often arranged in rotating repetitions (*top row*), longer passages (*middle row*) are arranged spiraling round from the outside, often starting at the bottom right corner (*bottom row*).

Praise be to God

Muhammad

Ali

Allah - Muhammad - Ali

Surat al-Ikhlās - chapter 112 of the Quran

Surat al-Fātiha - first chapter of the Quran

5

4

3

2

1

BRAIDED BORDERS

Gilded interlaced borders are frequently found in the Islamic arts of the book. They are used to frame central geometric panels in frontispieces, section, and chapter titles throughout a work and, on occasion, whole pages of text, particularly in illuminated Qurans. One technique that is commonly used is to construct these braided borders on a simple grid of dots, often colored blue and red. The following selected examples are provided as an introduction and brief reference to such designs for aspiring illuminators.

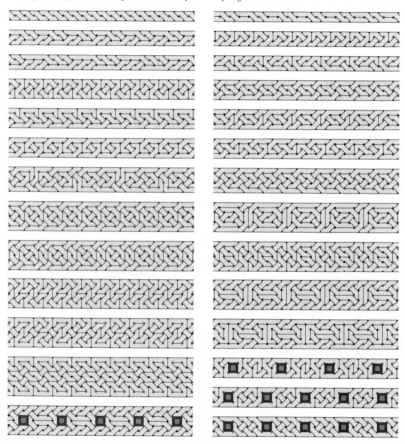